BRIT Wit

BRIT WIT

First published in 2005
Reprinted 2005, 2006, 2008, 2009, 2011
This abridged edition copyright © Summersdale Publishers Ltd, 2015

Illustrations by Ian Baker and Kath Walker

Summersdale Publishers Ltd
46 West Street
Chichester
West Sussex
PO19 1RP
UK

www.summersdale.com

Printed and bound in the Czech Republic

ISBN: 978-1-84953-665-3

Substantial discounts on bulk quantities of Summersdale books are available to corporations, professional associations and other organisations. For details contact Nicky Douglas by telephone: +44 (0) 1243 756902, fax: +44 (0) 1243 786300 or email: nicky@summersdale.com.

BRIT Wit

THE PERFECT RIPOSTE FOR EVERY SOCIAL OCCASION

SUSIE JONES

summersdale

CONTENTS

EDITOR'S NOTE

Winston Churchill was once voted the Greatest Briton of All Time in a BBC poll – but was he the wittiest? Make up your own mind as *Brit Wit* explores the many facets of the great British sense of humour so peculiar to this island and often unfathomable to those off it. Interspersed with cutting contributions from 'traditional' wits such as Samuel Johnson are ribald ripostes from modern sources – comedians, television presenters and, yes, even women. All of them unique, but all of them witty and typically British through their subtlety or cynicism. That is not to say that only the Brits have ever raised a wry smile. It was with great regret that Groucho Marx ('I never forget a face – but in your case I'll make an exception') and Dorothy Parker ('She runs the gamut of emotions from A to B', of Katharine Hepburn) had to stay out of this book!

So here you have it – the world with a pinch of salt. A Small Islander's guide to life, the universe and everything. Wow your friends, cow your enemies, and force yourself to see the funny side in a world that takes itself too seriously and not seriously enough. After all, as W. Somerset Maugham once observed, 'She had a pretty gift for quotation, which is a serviceable substitute for wit.'

Susie Jones

QUOTES AND QUOTATIONS

Find enough clever
things to say and you're
a Prime Minister;
write them down and
you're a Shakespeare.

GEORGE BERNARD SHAW

It is better to be quotable
than to be honest.

TOM STOPPARD

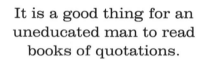

It is a good thing for an
uneducated man to read
books of quotations.

WINSTON CHURCHILL

A widely read man never quotes
accurately… misquotation is the
pride and privilege of the learned.

HESKETH PEARSON

The nicest thing about quotes
is that they give us a nodding
acquaintance with the originator,
which is often socially impressive.

KENNETH WILLIAMS

● ● ●

You cram these words
into mine ears against the
stomach of my sense.

WILLIAM SHAKESPEARE

A facility for quotation covers
the absence of original thought.

DOROTHY L. SAYERS

———•••———

I pick my favourite quotations
and store them in my mind
as ready armour, offensive or
defensive, amid the struggle
of this turbulent existence.

ROBERT BURNS

INSULTS

I fart in your
general direction.

FRENCH SOLDIER IN *MONTY PYTHON AND THE HOLY GRAIL*

Your brain is like the four-headed
man-eating haddock-fish beast
of Aberdeen. It doesn't exist.

EDMUND BLACKADDER IN *BLACKADDER*

What a tiresome affected sod.

NOËL COWARD ON OSCAR WILDE

Unreconstructed wankers.

TONY BLAIR ON THE SCOTTISH MEDIA

How tartly that gentleman looks!
I never can see him but I am
heart-burned an hour after.

WILLIAM SHAKESPEARE

The haste of a fool is the
slowest thing in the world.

THOMAS SHADWELL

A stupid man's report of what
a clever man says can never be
accurate, because he unconsciously
translates what he hears into
something he can understand.

BERTRAND RUSSELL

He is morally insensitive and
aesthetically disgusting.

GEORGE ORWELL ON RUDYARD KIPLING

O, she is the antidote to desire.

WILLIAM CONGREVE

A man who looks like a sexually
confused, ageing hairdresser: the
Teasy Weasy of Fleet Street.

RICHARD LITTLEJOHN ON PEREGRINE WORSTHORNE

He owes his celebrity
merely to his antiquity.

LORD BYRON ON GEOFFREY CHAUCER

Sir, you are like a pin, but without
either its head or its point.

DOUGLAS JERROLD

You look wise. Pray
correct that error.

CHARLES LAMB

He can't see a belt without hitting below it.

MARGOT ASQUITH ON DAVID LLOYD GEORGE

No one can have a higher opinion
of him than I have, and I think
he's a dirty little beast.

W. S. GILBERT

⎯⎯⎯●●●⎯⎯⎯

Of all the bulls that live, this
hath the greatest ass's ears.

QUEEN ELIZABETH I

⎯⎯⎯●●●⎯⎯⎯

You beat your pate, and
fancy wit will come;
Knock as you please,
there's nobody at home.

ALEXANDER POPE

Leonardo DiCaprio is patently
the result of an unnatural act of
passion between William Hague
and the piglet from *Babe*.

A. A. GILL

She is a peacock in
everything but beauty.

OSCAR WILDE

Like the British Constitution, she
owes her success in practice to
her inconsistencies in principle.

THOMAS HARDY

He'd be out of his depth
on a wet pavement.

JOE O'SHEA

RIPOSTES

A fly, sir, may sting a stately horse, and make him wince; but one is but an insect, and the other is a horse still.

SAMUEL JOHNSON

God forgive you, but I never can.

QUEEN ELIZABETH I TO THE COUNTESS OF NOTTINGHAM

Your wit's too hot, it speeds
too fast, 'twill tire.

WILLIAM SHAKESPEARE

One wit, like a knuckle ham in
soup, gives a zest and flavour
to the dish, but more than one
serves only to spoil the pottage.

TOBIAS GEORGE SMOLLETT

I refuse to answer that
question on the grounds that
I don't know the answer.

DOUGLAS ADAMS

You may be as vicious about
me as you please. You will
only do me justice.

RICHARD BURTON

WORK AND MONEY

I love deadlines. I especially like the whooshing sound they make as they go flying by.

DOUGLAS ADAMS

He says it's a
marvellous business…
In 30 years he's
never had a customer
ask for a refund.

HAL ROACH ON AN UNCLE'S BUSINESS AS AN UNDERTAKER

The first thing we do, let's
kill all the lawyers.

WILLIAM SHAKESPEARE

If you can't get a job as
a pianist in a brothel you
become a royal reporter.

MAX HASTINGS

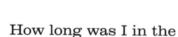

How long was I in the
army? Five foot eleven.

SPIKE MILLIGAN

One of the symptoms of an
approaching nervous breakdown
is the belief that one's work
is terribly important.

BERTRAND RUSSELL

I like work: it fascinates me. I
can sit and look at it for hours.

JEROME K. JEROME

Term, holidays, term, holidays,
till we leave school, and then
work, work, work till we die.

C. S. LEWIS

Asking a working writer
what he thinks about critics
is like asking a lamppost
how it feels about dogs.

CHRISTOPHER HAMPTON

———•●•———

Nothing is really work
unless you would rather be
doing something else.

J. M. BARRIE

———•●•———

I find it rather easy to portray
a businessman. Being bland,
rather cruel and incompetent
comes naturally to me.

JOHN CLEESE

Time is an illusion,
lunchtime doubly so.

DOUGLAS ADAMS

Make lots of money. Enjoy the
work. Operate within the law.
Choose any two of three.

JACK DEE

Idleness is only a coarse
name for my infinite capacity
for living in the present.

CYRIL CONNOLLY

There are three ways of losing
money: racing is the quickest,
women the most pleasant, and
farming the most certain.

LORD AMHERST

Anyone who lives within
their means suffers from
a lack of imagination.

ATTRIBUTED TO OSCAR WILDE

There's no money in poetry,
but then there's no poetry
in money, either.

ROBERT GRAVES

The only thing I like about rich people is their money.

NANCY ASTOR

The only reason I made a commercial for American Express was to pay for my American Express bill.

PETER USTINOV

When an actor comes to me and wants to discuss his character, I say, 'It's in the script.' If he says, 'But what's my motivation?' I say, 'Your salary.'

ALFRED HITCHCOCK

ADVICE

Human beings, who
are almost unique
in having the ability
to learn from the
experience of others,
are also remarkable
for their apparent
disinclination to do so.

DOUGLAS ADAMS

Never put a sock in a toaster.

EDDIE IZZARD

Never stand so high upon a principle that you cannot lower it to suit the circumstances.

WINSTON CHURCHILL

Contraceptives should be used on every conceivable occasion.

SPIKE MILLIGAN

Build a man a fire, and he'll
be warm for a day. Set a man
on fire, and he'll be warm
for the rest of his life.

TERRY PRATCHETT

A little inaccuracy sometimes
saves tons of explanation.

SAKI

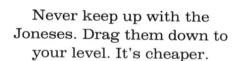

Never keep up with the
Joneses. Drag them down to
your level. It's cheaper.

QUENTIN CRISP

A sure cure for seasickness
is to sit under a tree.

SPIKE MILLIGAN

I always pass on good advice.
It's the only thing to do with it.
It is never any use to oneself.

OSCAR WILDE

If you're going to make rubbish,
be the best rubbish in it.

RICHARD BURTON

I asked my doctor what
I should do after having
a pacemaker put in.
He said, 'Keep paying
your electricity bill.'

ROGER MOORE

In university they don't tell you
that the greater part of the law
is learning to tolerate fools.

DORIS LESSING

⸺ ●●● ⸺

Success is a great deodorant. It
takes away all your past smells.

ELIZABETH TAYLOR

POLITICS

The best argument
against democracy
is a five-minute
conversation with
the average voter.

WINSTON CHURCHILL

Politics is supposed to
be the second oldest
profession. I have
come to realise that
it bears a very close
resemblance to the first.

RONALD REAGAN

In war, you can only be killed
once, but in politics, many times.

WINSTON CHURCHILL

———•●•———

Politics are usually the executive
expression of human immaturity.

VERA BRITTAIN

———•●•———

Despotism tempered
by assassination.

LORD REITH ON THE BEST FORM OF GOVERNMENT

Euphemisms are unpleasant truths
wearing diplomatic cologne.

QUENTIN CRISP

We know what happens to
people who stay in the middle of
the road. They get run over.

ANEURIN BEVAN

Being an MP is the sort of
job all working-class parents
want for their children – clean,
indoors and no heavy lifting.

DIANE ABBOTT

The President is a cross-eyed Texan warmonger, unelected, inarticulate, who epitomises the arrogance of American foreign policy.

BORIS JOHNSON ON GEORGE W. BUSH

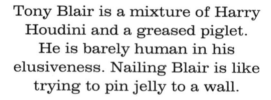

Tony Blair is a mixture of Harry Houdini and a greased piglet. He is barely human in his elusiveness. Nailing Blair is like trying to pin jelly to a wall.

BORIS JOHNSON

We started trying to set up a small anarchist community, but the people wouldn't obey the rules.

ALAN BENNETT

We all know that Prime Ministers
are wedded to the truth, but
like other married couples
they sometimes live apart.

SAKI

The Labour Party has lost the last
four elections. If they lose another,
they get to keep the Liberal Party.

CLIVE ANDERSON

If liberty means anything at all,
it means the right to tell people
what they don't want to hear.

GEORGE ORWELL

Politics is the enemy of
the imagination.

IAN MCEWAN

———————●●●———————

Democracy means government
by the uneducated, while
aristocracy means government
by the badly educated.

G. K. CHESTERTON

SPORT

Sudden success in
golf is like the sudden
acquisition of wealth.
It is apt to unsettle
and deteriorate
the character.

P. G. WODEHOUSE

In politics, if you want anything said, ask a man. If you want something done, ask a woman.

MARGARET THATCHER

Politicians. Little tin gods on wheels.

RUDYARD KIPLING

The difference between a misfortune and a calamity? If Gladstone fell into the Thames, it would be a misfortune. But if someone dragged him out again, it would be a calamity.

BENJAMIN DISRAELI

A Foreign Secretary is forever
poised between the cliché
and the indiscretion.

HAROLD MACMILLAN

Laws are generally found to be
nets of such a texture as the
little creep through, the great
break through, and the middle-
sized are alone entangled in.

WILLIAM SHENSTONE

There is no art which one
government sooner learns
of another than that of
draining money from the
pockets of the people.

ADAM SMITH

I became a great runner because
if you're a kid in Leeds and your
name is Sebastian you've got
to become a great runner.

SEBASTIAN COE

The only athletic sport I ever
mastered was backgammon.

DOUGLAS JERROLD

Ally MacLeod thinks that tactics
are a new kind of mint.

BILLY CONNOLLY

When I first met him [David Beckham] I didn't know whether to shake his hand or lick his face.

ROBBIE WILLIAMS

Oh God! If there be cricket in heaven let there also be rain.

ALEC DOUGLAS-HOME

The Oxford rowing crew – eight minds with but a single thought, if that.

MAX BEERBOHM

Watching Manchester City is probably the best laxative you can take.

PHIL NEAL

The place of the father
in the modern suburban
family is a very small one,
particularly if he plays golf.

BERTRAND RUSSELL

That's great, tell him he's
Pelé and get him back on.

JOHN LAMBIE, PARTICK THISTLE MANAGER, WHEN TOLD
A CONCUSSED STRIKER DID NOT KNOW WHO HE WAS

Golf, like measles, should
be caught young.

P. G. WODEHOUSE

Baseball has the great advantage over cricket of being sooner ended.

GEORGE BERNARD SHAW

I'd hate to be next door to her on her wedding night.

PETER USTINOV ON MONICA SELES

Michael Chang has all the fire and passion of a public service announcement, so much so that he makes Pete Sampras appear fascinating.

ALF RAMSEY

It's a funny kind of month, October. For the really keen cricket fan it's when you discover that your wife left you in May.

DENNIS NORDEN

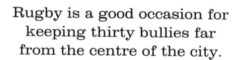

Rugby is a good occasion for keeping thirty bullies far from the centre of the city.

ATTRIBUTED TO OSCAR WILDE

We've lost seven of our last eight matches. Only team that we've beaten was Western Samoa. Good job we didn't play the whole of Samoa.

GARETH DAVIES ON THE WELSH RUGBY TEAM'S PERFORMANCE

Jogging is for people who
aren't intelligent enough
to watch television.

VICTORIA WOOD

I once jogged to the ashtray.

WILL SELF WHEN ASKED BY *THE IDLER* IF HE HAD EVER
HAD ANY ENCOUNTERS WITH SPORT AND EXERCISE

I tend to believe that cricket
is the greatest thing that God
ever created on earth... certainly
greater than sex, although
sex isn't too bad either.

HAROLD PINTER

RELIGION AND BELIEFS

The Bible tells us to love our neighbours, and also to love our enemies; probably because generally they are the same people.

G. K. CHESTERTON

To the philosophical eye the vices of the clergy are far less dangerous than their virtues.

EDWARD GIBBON

Heresy is another word for freedom of thought.

GRAHAM GREENE

It may be that our role on this planet is not to worship God, but to create him.

ARTHUR C. CLARKE

As the French say, there
are three sexes – men,
women and clergymen.

REVD SYDNEY SMITH

An atheist is a man who has no
invisible means of support.

JOHN BUCHAN

There is not in the universe a more
ridiculous, nor a more contemptible
animal, than a proud clergyman.

HENRY FIELDING

In the beginning the Universe
was created. This has made a
lot of people very angry and is
widely regarded as a bad move.

DOUGLAS ADAMS

Astrology proves one scientific
fact, and one only: there's
one born every minute.

PATRICK MOORE

I don't believe in astrology.
The only stars I can blame
for my failures are those that
walk about the stage.

NOËL COWARD

What would I like the sermon
to be about, vicar? I would like
it to be about ten minutes.

ARTHUR WELLESLEY

We have not lost faith, but we
have transferred it from God
to the Medical profession.

GEORGE BERNARD SHAW

It is the test of a good religion
whether you can joke about it.

G. K. CHESTERTON

We make guilty of our disasters
the sun, the moon, and the stars:
as if we were villains by necessity;
fools by heavenly compulsion.

WILLIAM SHAKESPEARE

The New Testament is
basically about what happened
when God got religion.

TERRY PRATCHETT

People are too apt to treat God
as if he were a minor royalty.

HERBERT BEERBOHM TREE

For Catholics, death
is a promotion.

BOB FOSSE

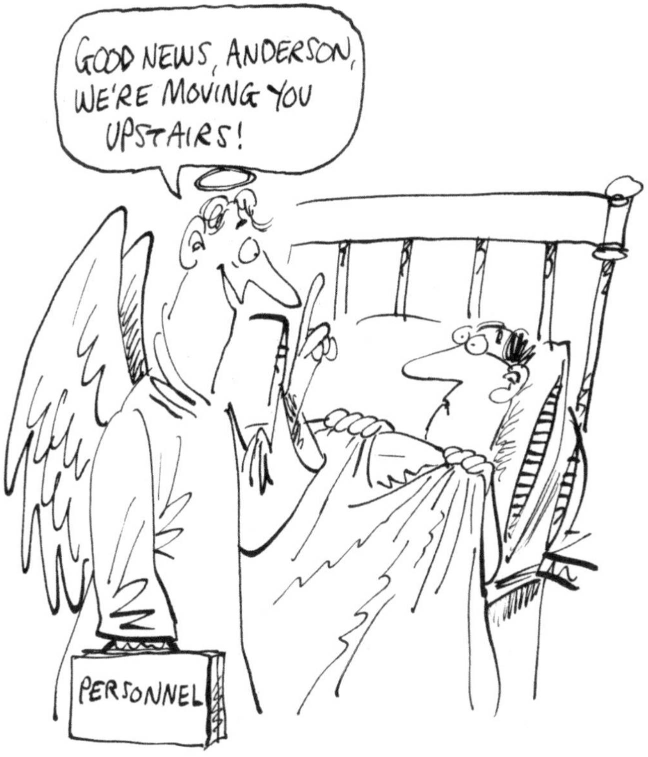
GOOD NEWS, ANDERSON, WE'RE MOVING YOU UPSTAIRS!
PERSONNEL

Man is made to adore and to
obey: but if you will not command
him, if you give him nothing
to worship, he will fashion
his own divinities, and find a
chieftain in his own passions.

BENJAMIN DISRAELI

For what a man would like to be
true, that he more readily believes.

FRANCIS BACON

Religion is something left
over from the infancy of
our intelligence, it will fade
away as we adopt reason and
science as our guidelines.

BERTRAND RUSSELL

Religion to me has always been the wound, not the bandage.

DENNIS POTTER

An honest God's the noblest work of man.

SAMUEL BUTLER

The Puritan hated bear-baiting, not because it gave pain to the bear, but because it gave pleasure to the spectators.

THOMAS BABINGTON MACAULAY

VICES AND VIRTUES

The unfortunate thing
about this world is that
the good habits are
much easier to give up
than the bad ones.

W. SOMERSET MAUGHAM

I hate people who think
it's clever to take drugs...
like customs officers.

JACK DEE

I have often wished I had time to
cultivate modesty. But I am too
busy thinking about myself.

EDITH SITWELL

If one sticks too rigidly to
one's principles, one would
hardly see anybody.

AGATHA CHRISTIE

I'm not against the police,
I'm just afraid of them.

ALFRED HITCHCOCK

The only way to get rid of a
temptation is to yield to it.

OSCAR WILDE

Minds, like bodies, will often fall
into a pimpled, ill-conditioned state
from mere excess of comfort.

CHARLES DICKENS

Follow your inclinations with
due regard to the policeman
round the corner.

W. SOMERSET MAUGHAM

No one gossips about other
people's secret virtues.

BERTRAND RUSSELL

I believe in getting into hot
water; it keeps you clean.

G. K. CHESTERTON

The law is like a woman's knickers – full of dynamite and elastic.

JOHN B. KEANE

People who can't be witty
exert themselves to be
devout and affectionate.

GEORGE ELIOT

The best car safety device is a
rear-view mirror with a cop in it.

DUDLEY MOORE

All charming people have
something to conceal, usually
their total dependence on the
appreciation of others.

CYRIL CONNOLLY

I don't have a drug problem.
I have a police problem.

KEITH RICHARDS

Virtue is like a rich
stone, best plain set.

FRANCIS BACON

I'm into pop because I want to get
rich, get famous and get laid.

BOB GELDOF

I was horrified to find the other week that my second son is taking drugs. My very best ones too.

BOB MONKHOUSE

He has all the virtues I dislike and none of the vices I admire.

WINSTON CHURCHILL ON STAFFORD CRIPPS

Commit the oldest sins, the newest kind of ways.

WILLIAM SHAKESPEARE

Her virtue was that she said what
she thought, her vice that what she
thought didn't amount to much.

PETER USTINOV

I have come to regard the
law-courts not as a cathedral
but rather as a casino.

RICHARD INGRAMS

WRITING, PUBLISHING AND MEDIA

There are books of
which the backs
and covers are by
far the best parts.

CHARLES DICKENS

This paperback is very
interesting, but I find it will never
replace a hardcover book – it
makes a very poor doorstop.

ALFRED HITCHCOCK

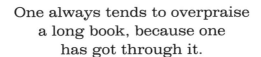

One always tends to overpraise
a long book, because one
has got through it.

E. M. FORSTER

The more I read him, the less I
wonder that they poisoned him.

THOMAS BABINGTON MACAULAY ON SOCRATES

If an Irishman says he's a writer, give him a sobriety test. If he flunks it he's telling the truth.

HENRY SPALDING

The work of a queasy
undergraduate scratching
his pimples.

VIRGINIA WOOLF ON *ULYSSES* BY JAMES JOYCE

As repressed sadists are supposed
to become policemen or butchers,
so those with irrational fear
of life become publishers.

CYRIL CONNOLLY

No news is good news; no
journalism is even better.

NICHOLAS BENTLEY

If you can't annoy somebody,
there's little point in writing.

KINGSLEY AMIS

A good novel tells us the truth
about its hero; but a bad novel tells
us the truth about its author.

G. K. CHESTERTON

Television thrives on unreason,
and unreason thrives on television.
It strikes at the emotions
rather than the intellect.

ROBIN DAY

The world may be full of fourth-rate writers, but it's also full of fourth-rate readers.

STAN BARSTOW

The quarrels of popes and kings, with wars and pestilences in every page; the men all so good for nothing, and hardly any women at all – it is very tiresome.

JANE AUSTEN ON HISTORY

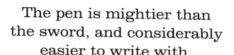

The pen is mightier than the sword, and considerably easier to write with.

MARTY FELDMAN

By increasing the size of the
keyhole, today's playwrights
are in danger of doing
away with the door.

PETER USTINOV

Somerset Maugham said there
were three rules for writing – and
nobody knows what they are.

JOAN COLLINS

Definition of a classic: a book
everyone is assumed to have read
and often thinks they have.

ALAN BENNETT

I have only read one book in my life and that is *White Fang*. It's so frightfully good I've never bothered to read another.

NANCY MITFORD

———— •●• ————

I can't understand these chaps who go round American universities explaining how they write poems; it's like going round explaining how you sleep with your wife.

PHILIP LARKIN

ENGLAND AND THE ENGLISH

You are offered a piece of bread and butter that feels like a damp handkerchief and sometimes, when cucumber is added to it, like a wet one.

COMPTON MACKENZIE ON AN ENGLISH TEA PARTY

But Lord! to see the absurd nature
of Englishmen, that cannot
forbear laughing and jeering at
everything that looks strange.

SAMUEL PEPYS

What a pity it is that we have
no amusements in England
but vice and religion!

REVD SYDNEY SMITH

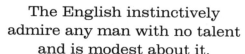

The English instinctively
admire any man with no talent
and is modest about it.

JAMES AGATE

We English are good at forgiving
our enemies; it releases us from
the obligation of liking our friends.

P. D. JAMES

The Welsh are so damn Welsh
that it looks like affectation.

ALEXANDER RALEIGH TO D. B. WYNDHAM LEWIS

The noblest prospect which a
Scotchman ever sees is the high-
road that leads him to England.

SAMUEL JOHNSON

This island is made mainly of
coal and surrounded by fish.
Only an organising genius
could produce a shortage of coal
and fish at the same time.

ANEURIN BEVAN

Dialect words – those
terrible marks of the beast
to the truly genteel.

THOMAS HARDY

He muffs his real job without
a blush, and yet he would
rather be shot than do his
bootlaces up criss-cross.

H. G. WELLS ON THE BRITISH OFFICER

I have been trying all my life
to like Scotchmen, and am
obliged to desist from the
experiment in despair.

CHARLES LAMB

The British electors will not vote
for a man who doesn't wear a hat.

LORD BEAVERBROOK'S ADVICE TO LORD DRIBERG

You have to give this much to
the Luftwaffe – when it knocked
down our buildings it didn't
replace them with anything more
offensive than rubble. We did that.

PRINCE CHARLES

The English Winter – ending in
July to recommence in August.

LORD BYRON

———•●•———

I like the English. They
have the most rigid code of
immorality in the world.

MALCOLM BRADBURY

The English never draw a
line without blurring it.

WINSTON CHURCHILL

When two Englishmen meet,
their first talk is of the weather.

SAMUEL JOHNSON

Britain is too small; if you have
a high-powered car to drive
around in it's like a roundabout.

WILL SELF

Kent, sir – everybody knows
Kent – apples, cherries,
hops and women.

CHARLES DICKENS

———————•●•———————

How amazing that the language
of a few thousand savages living
on a fog-encrusted island in
the North Sea should become
the language of the world.

NORMAN ST JOHN-STEVAS

COUNTRYSIDE
AND THE CITY

Anybody can be good in
the country. There are
no temptations there.

OSCAR WILDE

Clearly, then, the city is not a
concrete jungle, it is a human zoo.

DESMOND MORRIS

If you would be known, and
not know, vegetate in a village;
if you would know, and not
be known, live in a city.

CHARLES CALEB COLTON

When I am in the country I wish
to vegetate like the country.

WILLIAM HAZLITT

London, that great cesspool into which all the loungers of the Empire are irresistibly drained.

ARTHUR CONAN DOYLE

—•●•—

I have never understood why anybody agreed to go on being a rustic after about 1400.

KINGSLEY AMIS

My living in Yorkshire was so far out of the way, that it was actually 12 miles from a lemon.

REVD SYDNEY SMITH

I don't like the provinces. You can't eat and you can't get clean shirts.

MICK JAGGER

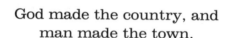

God made the country, and man made the town.

WILLIAM COWPER

No city should be too large for a man to walk out of in a morning.

CYRIL CONNOLLY

In my time, the follies of the
town crept slowly among us,
but now they travel faster
than a stage-coach.

OLIVER GOLDSMITH

I nauseate walking; 'tis a country
diversion, I loathe the country.

WILLIAM CONGREVE

God the first garden made,
and the first city Cain.

ABRAHAM COWLEY

A small country town is not the place in which one would choose to quarrel with a wife; every human being in such places is a spy.

SAMUEL JOHNSON

———— •●• ————

The great thing about Glasgow is that if there's a nuclear attack it'll look exactly the same afterwards.

BILLY CONNOLLY

OLD AGE

To get back my youth
I would do anything in
the world, except take
exercise, get up early,
or be respectable.

OSCAR WILDE

The older one grows, the
more one likes indecency.

VIRGINIA WOOLF

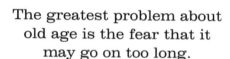

The greatest problem about
old age is the fear that it
may go on too long.

A. J. P. TAYLOR

Growing old is like being
increasingly penalised for a
crime you haven't committed.

ANTHONY POWELL

I want to be young and wild,
and then I want to be middle-
aged and rich, and then I want
to be old and annoy people
by pretending I'm deaf.

EDMUND BLACKADDER IN *BLACKADDER*

I refuse to admit that I am more
than 52, even if that makes
my children illegitimate.

NANCY ASTOR

Pushing 40? She's
hanging on for dear life.

IVY COMPTON-BURNETT

Youth tends to look ahead. Old age tends to look back. Middle age tends to look worried.

JAMES SIMPSON

At 50, everyone has the
face he deserves.

GEORGE ORWELL

———•••———

There is only one cure for
grey hair. It was invented
by a Frenchman. It is
called the guillotine.

P. G. WODEHOUSE

———•••———

Old age, believe me, is a good
and pleasant thing. It is true
you are gently shouldered
off the stage, but then you
are given such a comfortable
front stall as spectator.

JANE HARRISON

Time and trouble will tame
an advanced young woman,
but an advanced old woman is
uncontrollable by any earthly force.

DOROTHY L. SAYERS

Regrets are the natural
property of grey hairs.

CHARLES DICKENS

The years between 50 and
70 are the hardest. You are
always asked to do things,
and yet you are not decrepit
enough to turn them down.

T. S. ELIOT

Middle age is youth without levity, and age without decay.

DANIEL DEFOE

———— •●• ————

The past is the only dead thing that smells sweet.

CYRIL CONNOLLY

———— •●• ————

When you're my age you never risk being ill – because everyone says: oh, he's done for.

JOHN GIELGUD

An archaeologist is the best
husband a woman can have:
the older she gets, the more
interested he is in her.

AGATHA CHRISTIE

I have the body of an 18-year-old.
I keep it in the fridge.

SPIKE MILLIGAN

One of the many pleasures of
old age is giving things up.

MALCOLM MUGGERIDGE

Well, I suppose I must attribute it
to the fact that I haven't died yet.

MALCOLM SARGENT

———●●●———

Memorial services are the cocktail
parties of the geriatric set.

HAROLD MACMILLAN

———●●●———

We are happier in many ways
when we are old than when
we are young. The young sow
wild oats, the old grow sage.

WINSTON CHURCHILL

I can still rock like
a son of a bitch.

OZZY OSBOURNE

The long dull monotonous years
of middle-aged prosperity or
middle-aged adversity are excellent
campaigning weather for the Devil.

C. S. LEWIS

SCIENCE AND
TECHNOLOGY

Multimedia? As far
as I'm concerned,
it's reading with
the radio on!

RORY BREMNER

Reading computer manuals
without the hardware is as
frustrating as reading sex
manuals without the software.

ARTHUR C. CLARKE

Television is more interesting
than people. If it were not, we
should have people standing
in the corners of our rooms.

ALAN COREN

I have had my television aerials
removed. It's the moral equivalent
of a prostate operation.

MALCOLM MUGGERIDGE

Any sufficiently advanced
technology is indistinguishable
from magic.

ARTHUR C. CLARKE

—————•••—————

Television is like the invention
of indoor plumbing. It didn't
change people's habits. It just
kept them inside the house.

ALFRED HITCHCOCK

—————•••—————

Everything starts somewhere,
although many physicists disagree.

TERRY PRATCHETT

Technological progress has merely
provided us with more efficient
means for going backwards.

ALDOUS HUXLEY

The greatest task before
civilisation at present is to
make machines what they
ought to be, the slaves, instead
of the masters of men.

HAVELOCK ELLIS

A common mistake that
people make when trying to
design something completely
foolproof is to underestimate the
ingenuity of complete fools.

DOUGLAS ADAMS

Invention, it must be
humbly admitted, does not
consist of creating out of
void, but out of chaos.

MARY SHELLEY

———•●•———

The earth's crust is basically a
jerry-built botch of a job that no
structural surveyor would pass if
you applied for a mortgage on it.

HUGH DENNIS

I don't think necessity is the
mother of invention – invention,
in my opinion, arises directly
from idleness, possibly also from
laziness. To save oneself trouble.

AGATHA CHRISTIE

The email of the species is
more deadly than the mail.

STEPHEN FRY

YOUTH AND EDUCATION

Youth is a wonderful thing. What a crime to waste it on children.

GEORGE BERNARD SHAW

Young men think old men
are fools; but old men know
young men are fools.

GEORGE CHAPMAN

What is youth except a man
or a woman before it is
ready or fit to be seen?

EVELYN WAUGH

There is no sinner like
a young saint.

APHRA BEHN

Never lend your car
to anyone to whom
you have given birth.

ERMA BOMBECK

As a child, I thought I hated everybody, but when I grew up I realised it was just children I didn't like.

PHILIP LARKIN

———•●•———

Youth is wholly experimental.

ROBERT LOUIS STEVENSON

———•●•———

Teach him to think for himself? Oh my God, teach him rather to think like other people.

MARY SHELLEY ON HER SON'S EDUCATION

Universities incline wits to
sophistry and affectation.

FRANCIS BACON

Be on the alert to recognise
your prime at whatever time
of your life it may occur.

MURIEL SPARK

Getting an education was a bit
like a communicable sexual
disease. It made you unsuitable
for a lot of jobs and then you
had the urge to pass it on.

TERRY PRATCHETT

Age may have one side, but assuredly Youth has the other. There is nothing more certain than that both are right, except perhaps that both are wrong.

ROBERT BURNS

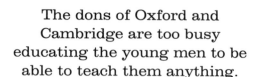

The dons of Oxford and Cambridge are too busy educating the young men to be able to teach them anything.

SAMUEL BUTLER

Education is the period during which you are being instructed by somebody you do not know, about something you do not want to know.

G. K. CHESTERTON

EATING AND DRINKING

Who discovered we could get milk from cows, and what did he THINK he was doing at the time?

BILLY CONNOLLY

Chopsticks are one of the
reasons the Chinese never
invented custard.

SPIKE MILLIGAN

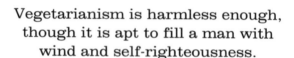

Vegetarianism is harmless enough,
though it is apt to fill a man with
wind and self-righteousness.

ROBERT HUTCHINSON

Good apple pies are a considerable
part of our domestic happiness.

JANE AUSTEN

Heaven sends us good meat,
but the Devil sends cooks.

DAVID GARRICK

The best number for a dinner
party is two – myself and a
damn good head waiter.

NUBAR GULBENKIAN

The salmon have got
their own back.

THE QUEEN MOTHER AFTER CHOKING ON A FISH BONE

All happiness depends on a leisurely breakfast.

JOHN GUNTHER

There are two types of women in this world, those who like chocolate and complete bitches.

DAWN FRENCH

I'm already two years ahead on my daily fat allowance. I'm looking for skinny people to see if I can borrow theirs.

JO BRAND

The proof that God has a very weird sense of humour is that, having invented the sublime mystery of haute cuisine, he went and gave it to the French.

A. A. GILL

No animal ever invented
anything so bad as drunkenness
– or so good as drink.

G. K. CHESTERTON

Claret is the liquor for boys; port
for men; but he who aspires to
be a hero must drink brandy.

SAMUEL JOHNSON

In 1969 I gave up drinking
and sex. It was the worst
20 minutes of my life.

GEORGE BEST

A tavern is a place where
madness is sold by the bottle.

JONATHAN SWIFT

•●•

Coffee in England always tastes
like a chemistry experiment.

AGATHA CHRISTIE

•●•

I like my coffee like I like my
women. In a plastic cup.

EDDIE IZZARD

Never drink black coffee
at lunch; it will keep you
awake all afternoon.

JILLY COOPER

Many, being reasonable,
must get drunk;
The best of life is
but intoxication.

LORD BYRON

LOVE, MARRIAGE AND SEX

A man... is *so* in the way in the house!

ELIZABETH GASKELL

No nice men are good
at getting taxis.

KATHERINE WHITEHORN

A woman's always younger
than a man of equal years.

ELIZABETH BARRETT BROWNING

Marriage is a wonderful
invention. But, then again,
so is the bicycle repair kit.

BILLY CONNOLLY

Love is the delightful
interval between
meeting a beautiful
woman and deciding she
looks like a haddock.

JOHN BARRYMORE

She's the sort of woman who lives
for others and you can tell the
others by their hunted expression.

C. S. LEWIS

Men are people, just like women.

FENELLA FIELDING

The first time Adam had
the chance, he put the
blame on a woman.

NANCY ASTOR

We were happily married for eight months. Unfortunately, we were married for four and a half years.

NICK FALDO

I married beneath me
– all women do.

NANCY ASTOR

Though women are angels,
yet wedlock's the devil!

LORD BYRON

I have met with women whom
I really think would like to
be married to a poem, and to
be given away by a novel.

JOHN KEATS

Advice to persons about
to marry – 'Don't.'

HENRY MAYHEW

Instead of getting married again,
I'm going to find a woman I don't
like and just give her a house.

ROD STEWART

Laugh and the world laughs with you. Snore and you sleep alone.

ANTHONY BURGESS

Marriage is the result of the longing for the deep, deep peace of the double bed after the hurly-burly of the chaise-longue.

MRS PATRICK CAMPBELL

Marriage is at best a dangerous experiment.

THOMAS LOVE PEACOCK

When a man opens the car
door for his wife, it's either
a new car or a new wife.

PRINCE PHILIP, DUKE OF EDINBURGH

It destroys one's nerves
to be amiable every day to
the same human being.

BENJAMIN DISRAELI

Many a good hanging
prevents a bad marriage.

WILLIAM SHAKESPEARE

We invite people like that to
tea, but we don't marry them.

LADY CHETWODE ON HER FUTURE SON-IN-LAW JOHN BETJEMAN

Love's like the measles – all the
worse when it comes late in life.

DOUGLAS JERROLD

To fall in love you have to
be in the state of mind for
it to take, like a disease.

NANCY MITFORD

One should always be in
love. That is the reason one
should never marry.

OSCAR WILDE

Marriage is an adventure,
like going to war.

G. K. CHESTERTON

[Dancing is] a perpendicular
expression of a horizontal desire.

GEORGE BERNARD SHAW

For a long time, I thought coq
au vin meant love in a lorry.

VICTORIA WOOD

I can still enjoy sex at 74 – I
live at 75 so it's no distance.

BOB MONKHOUSE

The tragedy is when you've
got sex in the head instead
of down where it belongs.

D. H. LAWRENCE

—•••—

Show me a man who loves football
and nine times out of ten you'll
be pointing at a really bad shag.

JULIE BURCHILL

FAMILIES
AND FRIENDS

A family is a tyranny
ruled over by its
weakest member.

GEORGE BERNARD SHAW

We make our friends; we make
our enemies; but God makes
our next-door neighbour.

G. K. CHESTERTON

Money couldn't buy friends, but
you get a better class of enemy.

SPIKE MILLIGAN

Parents are the bones upon which
children sharpen their teeth.

PETER USTINOV

But there, everything has its
drawbacks, as the man said
when his mother-in-law died,
and they came down upon him
for the funeral expenses.

JEROME K. JEROME

Gentlemen with broad chests and
ambitious intentions do sometimes
disappoint their friends by failing
to carry the world before them.

T. S. ELIOT

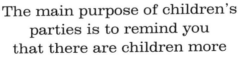

The main purpose of children's
parties is to remind you
that there are children more
awful than your own.

KATHERINE WHITEHORN

I've got more paternity
suits than leisure suits.

ENGELBERT HUMPERDINCK

Old friends are best. King James
used to call for his old shoes;
they were easiest for his feet.

JOHN SELDEN

Don't hold your parents up to
contempt. After all, you are
their son, and it is just possible
that you may take after them.

EVELYN WAUGH

Honolulu – it's got everything.
Sand for the children, sun for the
wife, sharks for the wife's mother.

KEN DODD

Many a man who thinks to found a
home discovers that he has merely
opened a tavern for his friends.

NORMAN DOUGLAS

My father was frightened of
his mother. I was frightened
of my father, and I'm damned
well going to make sure that my
children are frightened of me.

KING GEORGE V

Friends are God's apology
for relations.

HUGH KINGSMILL

The family – that dear
octopus from whose tentacles
we never quite escape.

DODIE SMITH

———•●•———

Friends are thieves of time.

FRANCIS BACON

———•●•———

It is a melancholy truth
that even great men have
their poor relations.

CHARLES DICKENS

Before I got married I had
six theories about bringing
up children; now I have six
children, and no theories.

JOHN WILMOT

I have never understood this
liking for war. It panders
to instincts already well
catered for in any respectable
domestic establishment.

ALAN BENNETT

After all, what is a pedestrian?
He is a man who has two cars –
one being driven by his wife, the
other by one of his children.

ROBERT BRADBURY

I've always been interested in
people, but I've never liked them.

W. SOMERSET MAUGHAM

The real art of conversation
is not only to say the right
thing in the right place but to
leave unsaid the wrong thing
at the tempting moment.

LADY DOROTHY NEVILL

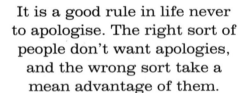

It is a good rule in life never
to apologise. The right sort of
people don't want apologies,
and the wrong sort take a
mean advantage of them.

P. G. WODEHOUSE

Incessant company is as bad
as solitary confinement.

VIRGINIA WOOLF

Dontopedology is the science
of opening your mouth and
putting your foot in it. I've
been practising it for years.

PRINCE PHILIP, DUKE OF EDINBURGH

The trouble with her is that she
lacks the power of conversation
but not the power of speech.

GEORGE BERNARD SHAW

A person who is keen to
shake your hand usually has
something up his sleeve.

ALEC GUINNESS

Never say a humorous thing
to a man who does not possess
humour. He will always use
it in evidence against you.

HERBERT BEERBOHM TREE

The penalty for success is
to be bored by the people
who used to snub you.

NANCY ASTOR

I am patient with stupidity but not
with those who are proud of it.

EDITH SITWELL

It is a common delusion
that you make things better
by talking about them.

DAME ROSE MACAULAY

Unless one is a genius, it is best
to aim at being intelligible.

ANTHONY HOPE HAWKINS

In my mind, there is nothing
so illiberal and so ill-bred,
as audible laughter.

LORD CHESTERFIELD

———————•●•———————

The aim of a joke is not to degrade
the human being but to remind
him that he is already degraded.

GEORGE ORWELL

'Know thyself' is a most
superfluous direction. We can't
avoid it. We can only hope
that no one else knows.

IVY COMPTON-BURNETT

———— • ● • ————

Never seem more learned than
the people you are with. Wear
your learning like a pocket watch
and keep it hidden. Do not pull it
out to count the hours, but give
the time when you are asked.

LORD CHESTERFIELD

CULTURE

No opera plot can
be sensible, for in
sensible situations
people do not sing.

W. H. AUDEN

Beethoven always sounds to
me like the upsetting of a bag
of nails, with here and there
an also dropped hammer.

JOHN RUSKIN

The English are not very spiritual
people, so they invented cricket to
give them some idea of eternity.

GEORGE BERNARD SHAW

The harpsichord sounds like
two skeletons copulating
on a corrugated iron roof
– in a thunderstorm.

THOMAS BEECHAM

His vibrato sounded like he
was driving a tractor over a
ploughed field with weights
tied to his scrotum.

SPIKE MILLIGAN

———————•●•———————

I couldn't warm to Chuck Berry
even if I was cremated next to him.

KEITH RICHARDS

———————•●•———————

Music-hall songs provide the
dull with wit, just as proverbs
provide them with wisdom.

W. SOMERSET MAUGHAM

People are wrong when they say
that opera is not what it used
to be. It *is* what it used to be.
That is what is wrong with it.

NOËL COWARD

The remarkable thing about
Shakespeare is that he really
is very good, in spite of all the
people who say he is very good.

ROBERT GRAVES

I think that a lifetime of listening
to disco music is a high price to
pay for one's sexual preference.

QUENTIN CRISP

Education... has produced a
vast population able to read
but unable to distinguish
what is worth reading.

G. M. TREVELYAN

———————— •●• ————————

Art consists of limitation.
The most beautiful part of
every picture is the frame.

G. K. CHESTERTON

LIFE

The important thing
when you are going to
do something brave
is to have someone on
hand to witness it.

MICHAEL HOWARD

When an opera star
sings her head off,
she usually improves
her appearance.

VICTOR BORGE

Don't be afraid to take big
steps. You can't cross a
chasm in two small jumps.

DAVID LLOYD GEORGE

• ● •

Blessed is the man who, having
nothing to say, abstains from
giving wordy evidence of the fact.

GEORGE ELIOT

• ● •

If you can't be a good example,
then you'll just have to be
a horrible warning.

CATHERINE AIRD

Better keep your mouth shut
and be thought a fool than
open it and remove all doubt.

DENIS THATCHER

If you are cast in a different
mould to the majority, it is no
merit of yours: Nature did it.

CHARLOTTE BRONTË

Sometimes one likes foolish
people for their folly, better than
wise people for their wisdom.

ELIZABETH GASKELL

When all is said and done,
monotony may after all be the
best condition for creation.

MARGARET SACKVILLE

———•●•———

It is dangerous to be sincere
unless you are also stupid.

GEORGE BERNARD SHAW

———•●•———

Drama is life with the
dull bits cut out.

ALFRED HITCHCOCK

Life is like a tin of sardines. We
are all looking for the key.

ALAN BENNETT

You should make a point of trying
every experience once, excepting
incest and folk-dancing.

ARNOLD BAX

One of the universal rules of
happiness is: always be wary
of any helpful item that weighs
less than its operating manual.

TERRY PRATCHETT

People tell me I'm
a legend. In other
words, a has-been.

BOB DYLAN

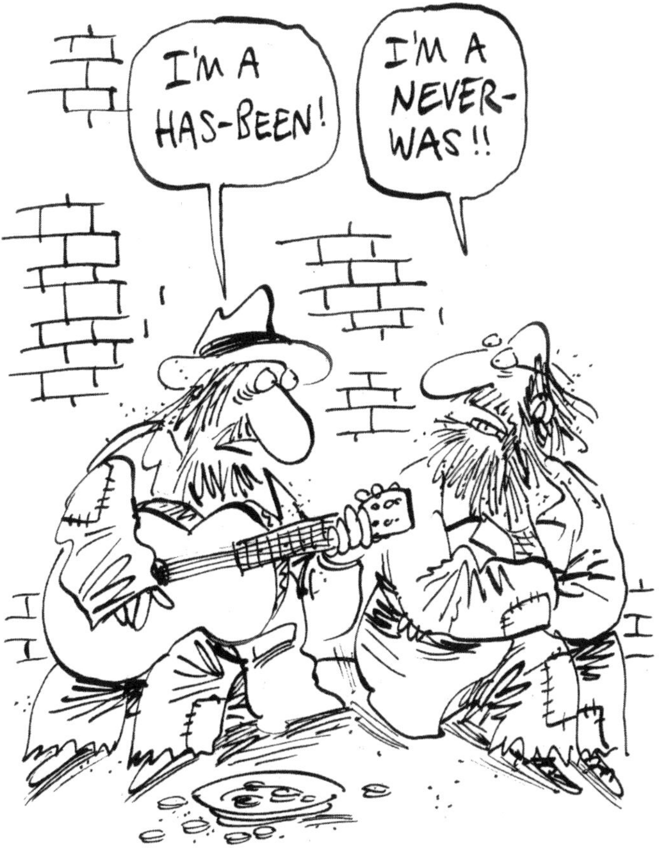
I'M A HAS-BEEN!
I'M A NEVER-WAS!!

The place where optimism most flourishes is the lunatic asylum.

HAVELOCK ELLIS

One might well say that mankind is divisible into two great classes: hosts and guests.

MAX BEERBOHM

DEATH

Dying is a very dull,
dreary affair. And
my advice to you
is to have nothing
whatever to do with it.

W. SOMERSET MAUGHAM

An optimist is someone
on Death Row who's
also a member of
Weight Watchers.

KEVIN FLYNN

You have to be a bastard to
make it, and that's a fact.
And the Beatles are the
biggest bastards on earth.

JOHN LENNON

For what do we live, but to make
sport for our neighbours, and
laugh at them in our turn?

JANE AUSTEN

Reality leaves a lot to
the imagination.

JOHN LENNON

Be happy while you're living,
for you're a long time dead.

SCOTTISH PROVERB

Death seems to provide the minds
of the Anglo-Saxon race with
a greater fund of amusement
than any other single subject.

DOROTHY L. SAYERS

Autobiography: an obituary
in serial form with the last
instalment missing.

QUENTIN CRISP

At my age I do what Mark Twain
did. I get my daily paper, look
at the obituaries page and if I'm
not there I carry on as usual.

PATRICK MOORE

———•••———

There is nothing quite so good as
burial at sea. It is simple, tidy,
and not very incriminating.

ALFRED HITCHCOCK

———•••———

I shall not waste my days in
trying to prolong them.

IAN FLEMING

I am ready to meet my Maker.
Whether my Maker is prepared
for the great ordeal of meeting
me is another matter.

WINSTON CHURCHILL

If this is dying, then I
don't think much of it.

LYTTON STRACHEY

Death comes along like a
gas bill one can't pay.

ANTHONY BURGESS

Something which everyone
reaches at the rate of
60 minutes an hour.

C. S. LEWIS ON THE FUTURE

————●●●————

If you do not think about your
future, you cannot have one.

JOHN GALSWORTHY

Man is the only animal that
can remain on friendly terms
with the victims he intends
to eat until he eats them.

SAMUEL BUTLER

I blame myself for my
boyfriend's death. I shot him.

JO BRAND

This is the first age that's
paid much attention to the
future, which is a little ironic
since we may not have one.

ARTHUR C. CLARKE

If you're interested in finding
out more about our books,
find us on Facebook at
Summersdale Publishers
and follow us on Twitter at
@Summersdale.

www.summersdale.com